Big Vegan Bowl Cookbook

70 One-Dish Vegan Meals, Healthy Breakfasts, Salads, Quinoa, Smoothies and Desserts High-protein Recipes

Joseph P. Turner

Copyright © All Right Reserved.

No part of this publication may be reproduced, distributed, or transmitted in any form or by any means, including photocopying, recording, or other electronic or mechanical methods, or by any information storage and retrieval system without the prior written permission of the publisher, except in the case of very brief quotations embodied in critical reviews and certain other noncommercial uses permitted by copyright law.

DISCLAIMER

The information provided in this program is for educational purposes only. The author is not a doctor and this information shouldn't be taken as medical advice. You should get a physician's approval before attempting any of the information in this program. This program is designed for healthy adults of 18 years and older. If you have any existing injuries, conditions or health issues, please seek your physician's approval before attempting any type of information in this program. The author is not liable or responsible for any damages, resulting from the use of this program. The user acknowledges any risk of injury, caused or alleged, with the use of this information. If your physician advises to not use the information provided in the program, please abide by those orders.

Always seek the advice of your physician or another qualified health provider with any questions you may have regarding a medical condition. Never disregard professional medical advice or delay seeking it because of something you have read here. Full medical clearance from a licensed physician should be obtained before beginning or modifying any diet, exercise, or lifestyle program, and your physician should be informed of all nutritional changes.

YOUR FREE GIFT

As a way of saying thanks for your purchase, I'm offering a free bonus book «**How Vegans Get Calcium, Iron, Zinc, Phosphorus, Vitamins A, B12, C & D: Mineral & Vitamin Deficiencies on a Vegan Diet and How to Fix Them**»

GET THE LINK AT THE END OF THE BOOK

TABLE OF CONTENTS

Introduction 7
    What is "Food in Bowls" trend? 7
    How did it get its name? 7
    Why a bowl? 7
    Why Has the Food Bowl Trend Become So Popular? 8
    What is the Buddha bowl? 8
BREAKFAST 10
    Almond Queen Fruit Smoothie 10
    Breakfast Almond Granola 12
    Brown Rice Almond Porridge (Instant Pot) 13
    Buckwheat Chocolate Granola 14
    Cauliflower Sesame Bowl 16
    Cauliflower Smoothie Bowl 17
    Chia and Linseed Cream with Fruits 18
    Flax Porridge with Raspberries 19
    Instant Porridge with Blackberries and Apricot 20
    Polenta with Almond Butter and Berries 21
    Polenta with Mushrooms 22
    Pumpkin Oatmeal with Figs, Banana and Pecans 23
    Savory Polenta Breakfast Bowl 24
    Sweet Potato & Pecans Bowl 25
    Tropic Breakfast Bowl 27
    Vegan Apple Bran Granola (Slow Cooker) 28
L U N C H 29
    Baked Chickpeas with Tomato 29
    Buckwheat Pasta with Vegan Cashew Sauce 30
    Garlic Bread Salad 31
    Glass Noodles and Vegetables in Soy Sauce Bowl 32
    Herbed Bulgur Salad Bowl 34
    Korean Chilled Cucumber Soup 35

Lemon Rice with Cilantro and Avocado 36
Mexican Radishes - Avocado Salad 37
Mushrooms, Peas and Tofu Bowl 38
Peas and Potatoes Stew 39
Sour Rice and Avocado Salad 40
South American Salad Bowl 41
Spanish Veggie Salad Bowl 42
Toscan Panzanella Salad Bowl 44
Vegan Noodles with Pesto 46

DINNER 47
Artichoke Hearts with Rice Bowl 47
Broccoli Rabe, Crimini with Cannellini Beans Soup 48
Fried Beans with Tofu Cheese Bowl 49
Lenten Rice, Mushrooms and Lettuce Bowl 50
Oven-baked Rice Stuffed Zucchini 51
Penne Pasta with Avocado and Corn Salad 52
Peperonata - Southern Italian Pepper Salad 53
Red Cabbage Salad 54
Rice and Edamame with Citrus-Lime Vinaigrette Bowl 55
Roasted Brussels sprouts and Pumpkin Salad Bowl 56
Roasted Sweet Potato, Mushrooms & Pomegranate Bowl 58
Spicy Asian Soup Bowl 60
Sweet Potato Soup with Curry 62
Traditional Persian Shirazi Salad 63
Vegan Spicy Coconut Curry 64

SNACKS 65
Avocado Guacamole Bowl 65
Baked Corn - Cashews Dip 66
Broccoli Mustard Dip 67
Creamy Cherry Salsa with Almonds 68
Gluten-free Quinoa Bowl 69
Hearty Black Bean Spread 70
Instant Piquant Bean Dip 71

Italian Beans Hummus 72

Parsley and Pine Nuts Dip 73

Vegan Potato Salad 74

DESSERTS 75

Banana Apricot Cream Bowl 75

Coconut Cereals with Berry, Banana Bowl 76

Coconut Yogurt Parfait with Berries 77

Fruity Summer Smile Bowl 78

Healthy Cocoa - Chia Cream 79

Japanese Shaved Matcha Ice Dessert 80

Murky Acai Banana Bowl 81

Pumpkin Parfait with Coconut Nibs Bowl 82

Quinoa-Banana Monkey Bowl 83

Vegan 'Cotton Candy' Mousse 84

BRUNC H 85

Exotic Fruit Salad with Lime Syrup 85

Fruit Bowl with Poppy Seeds 86

Fruity Couscous Salad 87

Quinoa and Fruits Salad Bowl 88

Watermelon Fruit Salad Bowl 89

About the Author 90

Other Books by Joseph P. Turner 92

Introduction

Going on a diet boils down to swapping out the bad foods with the good foods and then shrinking the portion size. Vegan bowls fulfill both of those conditions and serve as a wonderful way to start a day. Thanks to their customizability, foods in bowls took the world by surprise.

What is "Food in Bowls" trend?

In 2016, foodie accounts on social networks started buzzing about the "food in bowls" trend. When the British royal wedding between Prince Harry and Meghan Markle showed food in bowls in 2018, the entire world was mesmerized by their simplicity and elegance, so the trend was born.

At first, it seemed the food in bowls trend will peter out, but it kept gaining momentum until even The Wall Street Journal commented on it, saying everything "from poached eggs to smoothies" is now acceptable to serve in a bowl. From hipster restaurants to upscale diners, the bowl has become a perfectly acceptable replacement for the plate.

Places like Upbeet serve healthy diets and good vibes on the go, with customers being able to customize their every meal. People wait in line to grab vegan and gluten-free dressings to top their salads, snap a couple of amazing photos and chow it down. Atlanta's Gusto is a fast food place that took food in bowls trend to the next level, with the plan to serve bowls to drive-thru customers.

Breakfasts can be served in bowls too, with everything from cereal to acai berries finding its place in a bowl. Atlanta's Vitality Bowls serves breakfast bowls with ginger, peanut butter, pineapples, mangos, and much more. Those with a sweet tooth can even toss in vegan chocolate chips.

As the trend keeps growing, we will likely see many more vegan-friendly restaurants and fast food places, helping spread awareness about ethical eating.

How did it get its name?

The "foods in bowls" trend got its name from trendsetters and food critics who couldn't fathom the trend but couldn't reject it either. Being so highly visible in the public eye, they tried to present the trend as something passing and unworthy of attention but were oh-so-wrong.

Everyone adopted the bowl, toying with the idea and showing us that meals can and should be fun and, most of all, portable. From toddler to elder, everyone embraced the bowl and made their variation of foods in bowls.

Why a bowl?

Imagine yourself at a party. You like to grab and to nibble on a few canapes shuttled around by servers in between conversations. With a bowl, all of these changes.

The main two advantages of foods in bowls are that they're harder to spill and allow the guests to keep mingling. The problem with high-brow gatherings is that guests have to be carefully seated, so everyone has a great time, but foods in bowls help the hosts avoid that hassle—every guest can mingle without going back to the table to eat or hunting down canapes.

The main disadvantage is that both hands are occupied, which prevents handshakes and holding a drink alongside the bowl. Still, spills are bound to happen, and newspapers reporting on the trend jokingly said that dry cleaners would be the ones profiting from it.

No matter the snickering, the trend keeps going and growing. In 2016, Business Insider reported the foods in bowls trend rose by nearly 30% since 2011. The rise of foods in bowls led to many variations on the trend, such as the Buddha Bowl. With foods in bowls, the eater becomes more mindful of what they're eating, properly chewing it and enjoying it, becoming almost Buddha-like.

Why Has the Food Bowl Trend Become So Popular?

The food bowl trend is starting to change the entire food industry from the ground up. Eaters of all ages fell in love with customization options and are ready to try all sorts of combinations. For food producers, this means they can start combining all sorts of foods and offer something for every palate.

The freedom of choice means texture, flavor, and macro-nutrients can be customized as well, allowing each person to eat exactly as many vitamins, minerals, and calories as they want. As a great bonus, all these bowls look so photogenic, leading to a massive wave of social media food bowl content and shares.

It's not surprising that the food bowl is, on average, much healthier than a random fast food meal. Customers can go with fresh veggies, some protein, and a sauce, eating tasty food and reducing their calorie intake. Restaurants and fast-food chains took note of the idea and starting offering salads that give them a menu that's more appealing to the health-conscious consumer.

In essence, food in a bowl is a deconstructed meal, but that's not necessarily bad. It turned out people really like knowing what they're eating, and food in a bowl gives them exactly what they want.

What is the Buddha bowl?

Buddha is commonly shown as having a pot belly, so a Buddha bowl shouldn't evoking the idea of a healthy meal in a bowl but wait until you see the ingredients. The Buddha bowl most commonly hosts brown rice or quinoa, beans, roasted or raw veggies, and various greens, making it one of the most filling meals imaginable.

Making a Buddha bowl comes down to getting inspired and finding just the right combination of ingredients that suits you. One variation calls for mushrooms with kale and a cashew-parsley pesto drizzle on top. If there's any sauce leftover, use it for vegan sandwiches. The original Buddha bowl recipe involves quinoa, olives, tomatoes, and avocado, with everything except quinoa, served raw for an extra helping of nutrients and 600 calories.

Chickpeas, shredded carrots, radishes, alfalfa sprouts, and cabbage also deserve to find their place in a Buddha bowl. Gluten-free vegan noodles are welcome to join the bowl party as well, with veggies packing an astounding flavor that boosts your metabolism and lets you greet the day happy, smiling, and with a full tummy.

BREAKFAST

ALMOND QUEEN FRUIT SMOOTHIE

Ready in Time: 10 minutes | Servings: 2

Ingredients

1 1/2 cup almond milk

1 small peeled banana cut into 1-inch chunks and frozen

1 cup frozen peaches, sliced, thawed

3 Tbsp toasted almonds ground

1 scoop protein powder (pea or soy)

1 Tbsp flaxseed (ground)

Instructions

1. Add all ingredients into a high-speed blender and blend until smooth.

2. Pour your smoothie into the bottle, glass, or Mason jars; cover and keep refrigerated up to 2 days.

3. Or, pour your smoothie into a freezer-safe Ziploc bag and freeze up to 3 months.

4. Let it defrost in the refrigerator overnight, stir and enjoy!

Nutrition Facts

Percent daily values based on the Reference Daily Intake (RDI) for a 2000 calorie diet.

Amount Per Serving

Calories 262 | Calories From Fat (26%) 67.61 | Total Fat 8g 12% |

Saturated Fat 0.7g 3% | Cholesterol 1.16mg <1% | Sodium 26.49mg 1% | Potassium 497.5mg 14% | Total Carbohydrates 45.27g 15% |

Fiber 5.6g 21% | Sugar 34.85g | Protein 6.58g 13%

Breakfast Almond Granola

Servings: 12 | Preparation Time: 40 minutes

Ingredients

4 Tbsp coconut oil melted

4 cups old-fashioned rolled oats

1 1/2 cups of shredded coconut

1 1/2 cups of sliced almonds

1/3 cup of Maple syrup or simple syrup

3/4 tsp ground cinnamon

pinch of salt

1 cup of golden raisins

Instructions

1. Preheat oven to 350 F/175 C.
2. Heat the coconut butter in a large baking sheet for about 5 minutes.
3. Remove from oven and add rolled oats, coconut, and almonds.
4. Drizzle with syrup and sprinkle with cinnamon and salt.
5. Bake for 25 to 30 minutes, stirring frequently.
6. Remove from oven; stir in raisins.
7. Cool completely before serving.
8. Keep stored in an airtight container.

Nutrition Facts

Calories 456.29 |Total Fat 19.5g 30% |Total Carbohydrates 61.68g 21%|Protein 13.16g 26%

Brown Rice Almond Porridge (Instant Pot)

Servings: 4| Preparation Time: 30 minutes

Ingredients

1 cup of brown rice, short-grain

3 cups of almond milk

4 Tbsp granulated brown sugar (or more as needed)

1 Tbsp almond butter (plain, unsalted)

1 Tbsp pure vanilla extract

Fruits and almonds for serving

Instructions

1. Rinse the rice with tap water and drain.

2. Add all ingredients into Instant Pot; stir well.

3. Lock lid into place and set on the MANUAL setting high pressure for 20 minutes.

4. When the timer beeps, press "Cancel" and carefully flip the Quick Release valve to let the pressure out.

5. Serve with fruits and almonds.

Nutrition Facts

Calories 256.17 | Total Fat 3.72g 6% | Total Carbohydrates 54.5g 18% | Protein 3.86g 8%

Buckwheat Chocolate Granola

Servings: 8 | Preparation Time: 50 minutes

Ingredients

2 cups of buckwheat flour, whole-groat

1 cup of sunflower seeds

1/2 cup of coconut flakes

1 cup of Dates cut into small pieces

4 Tbsp of vegetable oil

4 Tbsp Maple syrup

4 Tbsp cocoa powder

Pinch of salt

1 tsp cinnamon

1/2 tsp ground ginger

Instructions

1. Soak green buckwheat and the flower seeds for 20 to 30 minutes.
2. Drain, rinse, and dry on a paper towel.
3. Sprinkle with the coconut flakes, half dates, and stir.
4. Preheat oven to 360 F/180 C.
5. Line a baking sheet with parchment paper; set aside.
6. In a small saucepan, combine the oil, Maple syrup, cocoa powder, salt, cinnamon, and ginger.
7. Stir over medium-low heat for 2 to 3 minutes.
8. Pour the mixture into dry ingredients and stir well.
9. Arrange the mixture on a prepared baking sheet, and bake for 30-40 minutes; stir occasionally.
10. Transfer the granola into a bowl, add the remaining dates and stir well.
11. Keep in a glass jar.

Nutrition Facts

Calories 380 | Total Fat 17.17g 26% | Total Carbohydrates 53.71g 18% | Protein 7.58g 15%

Cauliflower Sesame Bowl

Servings: 4 | Preparation Time: 40 minutes

Ingredients

4 Tbsp olive oil

1 Tbsp ground cumin

1 large head of cauliflower, broken into bite-sized pieces

Salt and freshly ground black pepper

1/2 cup of sesame paste

2 cloves garlic, smashed and minced into a paste

Fresh juice of 1 lime

1/2 cup of water

Instructions

1. Preheat oven to 450 F/270 C.
2. Stir the olive oil, cauliflower florets, cumin, and the salt and pepper.
3. Arrange the cauliflower florets evenly onto a baking sheet.
4. Bake for about 25 to 30 minutes.
5. Stir the sesame paste, garlic, lime juice, and water in a small bowl.
6. Remove the cauliflower from the oven and transfer it in a large bowl.
7. Pout the sesame paste sauce over the cauliflower, and toss to combine well.
8. Serve warm.

Nutrition Facts

Calories 199.3 | Total Fat 19.4g 31% | Total Carbohydrates 5.11g 2% | Sugar 0.77g | Protein 2.37g 5%

Cauliflower Smoothie Bowl

Servings: 5 | Preparation Time: 15 minutes

Ingredients

2 cups of cauliflower rice

2 cups of almond or coconut milk

2 Tbsp cereals

2 small bananas, sliced

1/2 cup of applesauce

2 Tbsp coconut palm sugar

1 tsp nutmeg

1 tsp cinnamon

Fresh fruits and chopped nuts for serving

Instructions

1. Add all ingredients into a blender and blend until smooth.

2. Pour the mixture into a saucepan and heat up for 10 minutes over medium-low heat.

3. Top with fresh fruit and chopped nuts.

4. Serve warm.

Nutrition Facts

Calories 122.35 | Total Fat 0.61g <1% | Total Carbohydrates 25.53g 9% |Protein 2.23g 4%

CHIA AND LINSEED CREAM WITH FRUITS

Servings: 3 | Preparation Time: 15 minutes

Ingredients

1 1/2 cups of almond milk

3 Tbsp chia seeds

2 Tbsp linseed

1/3 cup of granulated sugar or to taste

4 Tbsp of coconut flakes

2 Tbsp of chopped nuts (any)

1/2 tsp cinnamon

Serving

Banana, passion fruit, strawberries, kiwi fruit

Instructions

1. Heat the almond milk in a saucepan over medium-high heat.

2. Stir in chia seeds and linseed, stir well and cook for 5 to 6 minutes.

3. Add the coconut flakes, nuts, and cinnamon; stir for a further one minute.

4. Taste and adjust sweetest to taste.

5. Serve warm with fresh fruits.

Nutrition Facts

Calories 265.48 | Total Fat 12.86g 20% | Total Carbohydrates 33.59g 11% | Protein 5.05g 10%

Flax Porridge with Raspberries

Servings: 6 | Preparation Time: 15 minutes

Ingredients

4 cups of almond milk or coconut milk

1 cups oat flakes

1 cup flax meal

1/2 cup shredded coconut

4 Tbsp granulated sugar

1 1/2 tsp cinnamon

1/2 cup almonds, chopped

1/2 cup of maple syrup or simple syrup

1 cup raspberries

Instructions

1. Heat the almond milk in a pot over medium-high temperature.
2. Stir in oats and the flax meal; reduce heat to medium and stir well.
3. Cook, occasionally stirring, for 5 to 6 minutes.
4. Stir in coconut flakes, sugar, and cinnamon; cook for one minute.
5. Stir in the almonds, stir and remove from heat.
6. Serve in a bowl.
7. Pour with the maple syrup, and decorate with fresh raspberries.

Nutrition Facts

Calories 514.5 | Total Fat 26.25g 40% | Total Carbohydrates 61.56g 21% | Protein 14.26g 29%

Instant Porridge with Blackberries and Apricot

Servings: 6 | Preparation Time: 15 minutes

Ingredients

2 cups oatmeal

6 cups of water

1 tsp pure vanilla extract

2 tsp ground cinnamon

2 cups blackberries

2 cups of apricots, peeled and sliced

1/3 cup of Maple syrup or simple syrup

3 to 4 Tbsp coconut yogurt or coconut cream for serving

Instructions

1. Add the oatmeal, water, vanilla, and cinnamon in your Instant Pot

2. Lock lid into place and set on the MANUAL setting for 7 minutes.

3. When the timer beeps, press "Cancel" and carefully flip the Quick Release valve to let the pressure out.

4. Transfer the oat mixture into bowls and cover with fruits.

5. Drizzle with the Maple syrup and toss to combine well.

6. Serve with coconut yogurt or coconut cream.

Nutrition Facts

Calories 276 | Total Fat 6.56g 10% | Total Carbohydrates 45.4g 15% | Protein 10.23g 20%

POLENTA WITH ALMOND BUTTER AND BERRIES

Servings: 4 | Preparation Time: 15 minutes

Ingredients

1 cup of corn flour

Pinch of salt

3 cups of water

1 large apple peeled and sliced

2 Tbsp almond butter

1/2 tsp cinnamon

1 cup of berries (any)

Instructions

1. Add water, corn flour, a pinch of salt, and cook, often stirring, for 7 to 8 minutes.

2. Stir in the almond butter and remove from heat.

3. Put in a bowl and garnish with cinnamon and berries; serve.

Nutrition Facts

Calories 185.83 | Total Fat 7.04g 11% | Total Carbohydrates 29.69g 10% | Protein 3.06g 6%

Polenta with Mushrooms

Servings: 6 | Preparation Time: 20 minutes

Ingredients

1 1/2 cups of polenta

4 cups of water

Salt and freshly ground black pepper to taste

1 Tbsp olive oil

2 chives

1 clove of garlic minced

2 cups of mushrooms champignon

1 1/2 cup of canned tomatoes

1 bunch of parsley chopped

1/2 tsp saffron

1 tsp thyme

Instructions

1. Cook polenta in salted water for about 4 to 5 minutes; stir often.

2. Remove from heat and pour into bowls.

3. Heat the oil in a frying skillet, and sauté chives and garlic for about 3 minutes.

4. Add the mushrooms, tomatoes, and parsley; cook for 5 minutes.

5. Add saffron, thyme, and season with the salt and pepper to taste.

6. Divide the mushroom mixture over polenta.

7. Serve immediately.

Nutrition Facts

Calories 295.23 | Total Fat 3g 5% | Total Carbohydrates 59.52g 20% | Protein 7.55g 15%

Pumpkin Oatmeal with Figs, Banana and Pecans

Servings: 3 | Preparation Time: 15 minutes

Ingredients

1 1/2 cup of almond milk

6 Tbsp oat flakes

3 Tbsp pumpkin puree

1/2 tsp cinnamon

1/4 tsp cardamom

1/4 tsp nutmeg

1 pinch of black pepper

Agave or Maple syrup to taste

For serving: figs, bananas, pecans

Instructions

1. Boil the milk in a saucepan with the oatmeal, pumpkin puree, and spices.
2. Cook over low heat, often stirring, until become soft.
3. Remove from heat, and allow it to cool down slightly.
4. Add syrup to taste and stir well.
5. Transfer the porridge into a bowl; decorate with figs, bananas, and pecans.
6. Sprinkle with cinnamon and serve.

Nutrition Facts

Calories 218.9 | Total Fat 8.3g 13% | Total Carbohydrates 34.07g 11% | Protein 4.41g 9%

Savory Polenta Breakfast Bowl

Servings: 6 | Preparation Time: 15 minutes

Ingredients

1 cup dry polenta

3 Tbsp nutritional yeast

2 cloves garlic minced

4 cups of water

Salt to taste

1/2 cup green onions chopped

1 can of black beans

1 avocado peeled, cut into cubes

1 cup of cherry tomatoes chopped

1 fresh lemon juice

Instructions

1. Combine the polenta, nutritional yeast, salt, and garlic in a medium mixing bowl.

2. Add water to a large pot, over medium-high heat, and boil.

3. Whisk in the polenta mixture and cook, often stirring, for about 4 to 5 minutes.

4. Spoon the polenta into bowls and top with the green onions, beans, avocado, and cherry tomatoes.

5. Drizzle with lemon juice and serve.

Nutrition Facts

Calories 321.34 | Total Fat 5.66g 9% | Total Carbohydrates 57.28g 19% | Protein 12.52g 25%

Sweet Potato & Pecans Bowl

Servings: 6 | Preparation Time: 40 minutes

Ingredients

1 cup of water

2 large sweet potatoes peeled, sliced

2 Tbsp coconut oil melted

1 cup of brown sugar

1 tsp vanilla extract

1 tsp cinnamon, ground

1/8 tsp nutmeg, ground

Topping

2 Tbsp almond butter (plain, unsalted) softened

1/3 cup sugar (brown or white, as you prefer)

1 Tbsp almond flour

1/3 cup pecans (chopped)

Instructions

1. Pour water to the inner stainless steel pot in the Instant Pot, and place the steam rack or a steamer basket; add sweet potato slices.

2. Lock lid into place and set on the MANUAL setting for 8 minutes.

3. When the timer beeps, press "Cancel" and carefully flip the Quick Release valve to let the pressure out.

4. Place sweet potatoes in a large bowl and stir in the brown sugar, vanilla, coconut oil, cinnamon, and nutmeg; stir to combine well.

5. Pour the sweet potato mixture into a greased casserole dish.

6. Preheat your oven to 350 F/175 C.

7. Stir the almond butter, brown sugar, flour, and nuts; pour evenly over the sweet potato mixture.

8. Bake for 12 to 15 minutes.

9. Serve hot.

Nutrition Facts

Calories 209.07 | Total Fat 11.88g 18% | Total Carbohydrates 25.6g 9% | Protein 1.95g 4%

Tropic Breakfast Bowl

Servings: 4 | Preparation Time: 15 minutes

Ingredients

1/2 small fresh pineapple, cut into cubes

2 large ripe bananas, sliced

1 red apple peeled and cut in small cubes (or shredded)

2 Tbsp shredded coconut

1 tsp nutmeg

1 tsp cinnamon

4 Tbsp almond butter softened

5 to 6 drops liquid sugar (or to taste)

Instructions

1. Place the pineapple cubes and banana slices in a large bowl.

2. Top with the apple, coconut, nutmeg, and cinnamon.

3. Stir the almond butter and liquid sugar; pour over the pineapple mixture and toss to combine well.

4. Serve.

Nutrition Facts

Calories 278.75 | Total Fat 10.3g 16% | Total Carbohydrates 47g 16% | Protein 4.89g 10%

VEGAN APPLE BRAN GRANOLA (SLOW COOKER)

Servings: 6 | Preparation Time: 4 hours and 5 minutes

Ingredients

2 Tbsp coconut oil melted

1 cup of oat flour

1 cup bran flakes

2 apples, cored and sliced

1/2 cup of apple juice

1/3 cup Maple syrup or simple syrup

A handful of chopped nuts

1 tsp nutmeg

1 tsp cinnamon

Pinch of salt

Instructions

1. Pour melted coconut oil into Slow Cooker

2. Add all remaining ingredients and give a good stir.

3. Cover and cook on LOW for 4 hours.

4. Transfer to a glass jar/bowl.

5. Keep refrigerated.

Nutrition Facts

Calories 186.4 | Total Fat 7.16g 11% | Total Carbohydrates 18.4g 6% | Protein 1.68g 3%

LUNCH

Baked Chickpeas with Tomato

Servings: 6 | Preparation Time: 1 hour

Ingredients

1 lb chickpeas, soaked overnight

Salt and freshly ground black pepper to taste

2 onions finely chopped

2 cloves of garlic minced

1 cup of grated tomatoes

1 cup of vegetable broth or water

1/2 cup of extra-virgin olive oil

3 sprigs of rosemary

2 bay leaves

2 small hot peppers, finely chopped

Instructions

1. Soak the chickpeas in lukewarm water for 8 hours or overnight.

2. Boil the chickpeas in salted water for 15 minutes over medium heat; drain.

3. Preheat oven to 380 F/190 C.

4. Add the chickpeas in a large baking dish with the onion, garlic, tomato, olive oil, and broth; stir to combine well.

5. Add the pepper, laurel leaves, rosemary, and some salt and freshly ground black pepper.

6. Place into the oven and bake for 40 to 45 minutes.

7. Serve warm.

Nutrition Facts

Calories 356 | Total Fat 5.65g 9% | Total Carbohydrates 61.12g 20% | Protein 17.86g 36%

Buckwheat Pasta with Vegan Cashew Sauce

Servings: 4 | Preparation Time: 25 minutes

Ingredients

10 oz buckwheat pasta

1 onion finely chopped

1 green bell pepper chopped

2 small carrots cut into strips

1 cup fresh mushrooms (portabella and shiitakes) sliced

3/4 cup of Vegan Cashew Sauce

2 Tbsp sesame oil

Instructions

1. Cook pasta as per manufactures instructions; rinse and drain.
2. In a large bowl, combine the pasta, onion, bell pepper, carrot strips, and mushrooms.
3. Pour with the Vegan Cashew Sauce and sesame oil; toss to combine well.
4. Serve.

Nutrition Facts

Calories 386.49 | Total Fat 8.21g 13% | Total Carbohydrates 65.4g 22% | Protein 13.18g 26%

Garlic Bread Salad

Servings: 4 | Preparation Time: 15 minutes

Ingredients

6 Tbsp extra virgin olive oil

11 oz white bread cut bite-sized dices

3 cloves of garlic minced

3 Tbsp pine nuts

1 Tbsp maple syrup

3 Tbsp balsamic vinegar

Salt and ground pepper to taste

1/2 cup of green olives pitted

1 large cucumber sliced

1/2 onion finely sliced

1/2 lb cherry tomatoes halved

1/2 cup of fresh basil chopped

Instructions

1. Heat 3 tablespoons oil in a pan and lightly toast the bread cubes with the garlic and pine nuts.

2. In a bowl, stir the remaining olive oil with the maple syrup and the vinegar; season to taste.

3. Combine all vegetables in a salad bowl and season with the salt and pepper to taste.

4. Top evenly with the bread mixture.

5. Serve.

Nutrition Facts

Calories 316.81 | Total Fat 27.17g 42% | Total Carbohydrates 17.83g 6% | Protein 4.33g 9%

Glass Noodles and Vegetables in Soy Sauce Bowl

Servings: 3 | Preparation Time: 20 minutes

Ingredients

8 oz glass noodles (sweet potato noodles or bean thread vermicelli)

4 oz spinach chopped

2 Tbsp peanut oil

1 Tbsp sesame oil

3 to 4 spring onions sliced

2 cloves garlic minced

1 carrot, cut into thin strips

4 to 5 Shiitake mushrooms sliced

Salt to taste

Sauce:

4 Tbsp soy sauce

2 Tbsp granulated sugar

Sea salt to taste

1 tsp sesame seeds for serving

Instructions

1. Cook the sweet potato noodles as per manufacturer's instruction.

2. Rinse noodles under cold running water; cut the noodles

3. Heat a pot of water and bring it to boil.

4. Blanch the spinach about one to two minutes; rinse and drain.

5. Make the spinach ball and cut it into half.

6. Heat the peanut oil in a frying skillet and sauté the spring onions, garlic, shiitake mushroom, and carrot, often stirring for about 3 to 4 minutes.

7. Add noodles, spinach, sesame oil, soy sauce, and sugar; toss to combine well.

8. Taste and season with the salt to taste.

9. Serve warm with sesame seeds.

Nutrition Facts

Calories 342.11 | Total Fat 16.28g 25% | Total Carbohydrates 44.3g 15% | Protein 7.22g 14%

Herbed Bulgur Salad Bowl

Servings: 5 | Preparation Time: 30 minutes

Ingredients

1/2 cup of bulgur

1 1/2 cup of water

1 cucumber cut into small cubes

3 tomatoes sliced

1 spring onion sliced

Salt to taste

1 cup of fresh parsley finely chopped (leaves)

1/2 cup of fresh mint chopped

6 Tbsp olive oil

Fresh juice from 2 lemons

Instructions

1. Cook bulgur with water in a saucepan for about 20 minutes.

2. Rinse and drain well.

3. Add all vegetables in a large salad bowl and season with the salt and pepper.

4. Add the bulgur and parsley and mint.

5. Drizzle with oil and lemon juice; toss to combine well.

6. Serve immediately.

Nutrition Facts

Calories 232.66 | Total Fat 16.83g 26% | Total Carbohydrates 19.4g 7% | Protein 3.52g 7%

Korean Chilled Cucumber Soup

Servings: 6 | Preparation Time: 15 minutes

Ingredients

1 cup of soaked seaweed or soybean sheets

2 cucumbers cut into thin match sticks.

1 green chili pepper finely chopped

2 Tbsp tamari sauce

2 Tbsp fresh lemon juice

1/2 tsp garlic minced or mashed

2 tsp sesame seeds toasted

1 tsp pepper flakes

4 cups of water

Sea salt to taste

Ice cubes for serving (optional)

Instructions

1. Boil water in a small pot, and add salt to taste.
2. Blanch the soaked seaweed or soybean sheets for 30 to 45 seconds; drain and rinse with water.
3. Drain again, squeeze out, and cut into small pieces.
4. Add in a large salad bowl along with all remaining ingredients.
5. Pour cold water and season to taste.
6. Refrigerate to chill well.
7. Serve cold.

Nutrition Facts

Calories 31 | Total Fat 0.69g 1% | Total Carbohydrates 6.08g 2% | Protein 1.42g 3%

Lemon Rice with Cilantro and Avocado

Servings: 4 | Preparation Time: 35 minutes

Ingredients

1 1/2 cups of long-grain rice

2 Tbsp olive oil

1/2 cup of chopped green onion

1 Tbsp minced garlic

2 3/4 cups of lukewarm water

2 Tbsp fresh lemon juice

Salt to taste

1/3 cup chopped cilantro

Avocado slices for serving

2 Tbsp sesame oil for serving (optional)

Instructions

1. Rinse the rice until the water comes out clear, drain, and set aside.
2. Heat oil in a large frying skillet over medium heat.
3. Sauté the onion and garlic with the pinch of salt for about 3 to 4 minutes.
4. Pour in water, one tablespoon of lemon juice, and bring to a boil over medium-high heat.
5. Add the rice, reduce heat to low, cover and simmer for approximately 18 to 20 minutes.
6. Remove from heat and let it rest, covered for 10 minutes.
7. Add the cilantro and the remaining one tablespoon lemon juice.
8. Drizzle with sesame oil, divide into cups, add the avocado slices and serve.

Nutrition Facts

Calories 405.6 | Total Fat 13.91g 21% | Total Carbohydrates 64.23g 21% | Protein 6.18g 12%

Mexican Radishes - Avocado Salad

Servings: 3 | Preparation Time: 10 minutes

Ingredients

6 radishes sliced

2 avocados, pitted and sliced

1 jalapeno chili pepper, sliced

4 Tbsp fresh cilantro finely chopped

4 Tbsp olive oil

2 Tbsp fresh lime juice

1 Tbsp liquid sweetener (any)

1/4 tsp ground cayenne pepper

1/4 tsp cumin

Kosher salt to taste

Instructions

1. Add radishes, avocado, jalapeno, and cilantro in a large salad bowl.

2. Whisk all remaining ingredients in a bowl and pour over the salad.

3. Serve immediately.

4. Keep refrigerated.

Nutrition Facts

Calories 371.17 | Total Fat 35.8g 55% | Total Carbohydrates 14.69g 5% | Protein 2.62g 5%

Mushrooms, Peas and Tofu Bowl

Servings: 4 | Preparation Time: 25 minutes

Ingredients

2 Tbsp olive oil

1 onion, sliced thinly

8 large white mushrooms, sliced

1 cup of sweet peas

1/2 lb extra firm tofu, drained, and cut into 1/2 inch cubes

2 tsp Curry powder

2 tsp coriander

1 tsp tamarind paste or molasses

1 tsp ground ginger

1 tsp ground turmeric

1/4 cup of fresh cilantro

Instructions

1. Heat oil in a large frying skillet; sauté the onion with the pinch of salt for 3 to 4 minutes.

2. Add in mushrooms, tofu cubes, and sweet peas, and cook for 3 minutes.

3. Add in all spices and cook, occasionally stirring, for 10 to 12 minutes.

4. Finally, add the chopped cilantro and stir to combine.

5. Taste and adjust the salt to taste.

6. Serve.

Nutrition Facts

Calories 337.8 | Total Fat 13.6g 21% | Total Carbohydrates 42.32g 14% | Protein 16.1g 32%

Peas and Potatoes Stew

Servings: 6 | Preparation Time: 45 minutes

Ingredients

3/4 cup of extra virgin olive oil

1 onion finely chopped

2 green onions, chopped

2 cloves of minced garlic

Salt and freshly ground pepper to taste

2 carrots thinly sliced

3 potatoes cut into cubes

1 1/2 cups grated tomatoes

2 cups of vegetable broth

1 Tbsp fresh basil chopped

16 oz peas (fresh or frozen)

1 Tbsp chives

Instructions

1. Heat the half olive oil in a large and deep pot.
2. Sauté the onion, green onion, and garlic with the pinch of salt until soft.
3. Add carrots, potatoes, and grated tomatoes and sauté for 3 minutes.
4. Pour in the vegetable broth, and bring to a boil; cook uncovered for 15 about minutes.
5. Add the peas, basil, and dill: and the remaining olive oil and season with salt and pepper to taste.
6. Stir well, lower the heat and simmer for about 12 minutes.
7. Serve warm.

Nutrition Facts

Calories 430.13 | Total Fat 28.14g 43% | Total Carbohydrates 40.14g 13% | Protein 6.65g 13%

Sour Rice and Avocado Salad

Servings: 4 | Preparation Time: 15 minutes

Ingredients

2 avocados

1 cup of long-grain rice cooked

1 cup of peas cooked

2 scallions finely sliced

1 cucumber sliced

1 carrot sliced

1/3 cup of extra virgin olive oil

2 Tbsp fresh lemon juice

Salt and pepper

Instructions

1. Cut avocado in half, remove the kernel with a knife, separate the flesh with a spoon, cut into thin slices.

2. Add rice into a bowl, and add rice, peas, scallions, cucumber, and carrot.

3. Season with the salt and pepper to taste; toss to combine well.

4. In a separate bowl, whisk the olive oil with the fresh lemon juice and a pinch of salt and pepper; pour it evenly over the salad.

5. Ready! Serve immediately.

Nutrition Facts

Calories 288.8 | Total Fat 14.33g 22% | Total Carbohydrates 36.8g 12% | Protein 6.54g 13%

South American Salad Bowl

Servings: 4 | Preparation Time: 35 minutes

Ingredients

1 large tomato diced

1 red onion sliced

2 Tbsp fresh cilantro leaves finely chopped

1 Tbsp chili pepper

Sea salt to taste

2 Tbsp of olive oil

2 cups sweet potato cut into cubes

1 tsp cumin

1 can (14 oz) of black beans, rinsed

3 cups of brown rice, cooked

1 avocado, sliced

Lemon or lime wedges for serving

Instructions

1. Combine the tomatoes, onion, cilantro, jalapeno, and salt in a medium bowl; toss to combine well.

2. Heat oil in a frying skillet over medium-high heat.

3. Add the sweet potato, cumin, and a pinch of salt.

4. Sauté for 5-7 minutes; stir occasionally.

5. Transfer the sweet potato to a bowl; set aside.

6. Warm the black beans in a small saucepan and arrange in a salad bowl.

7. Add the tomato mixture and all remaining ingredients.

8. Serve with lemon/lime wedges.

Nutrition Facts

Calories 312.44 | Total Fat 14.54g 22% | Total Carbohydrates 39.3g 13% | Protein 8.53g 17%

Spanish Veggie Salad Bowl

Servings: 5 | Preparation Time: 15 minutes

Ingredients

1 lettuce cut into strips

1/2 onion diced

1 carrot sliced

1 cup of celery finely chopped

1/2 red pepper sliced

1/2 green pepper sliced

1/2 cucumber sliced

1 cup olives pitted

Cherry tomatoes halved

Sea salt to taste

1 tsp sesame

1 tsp chia seeds

1 tsp sunflower seeds

Dressing:

1/3 cup of olive oil

2 Tbsp mustard

2 Tbsp apple vinegar

Instructions

1. Arrange the lettuce in a large salad bowl.

2. Add all remaining vegetables, and season with the salt to taste

3. In a separate bowl, whisk the dressing ingredients and pour over salad.

4. Finally, sprinkle with the sesame, chia and sunflower seeds.

5. Serve immediately.

Nutrition Facts

Calories 217.33 | Total Fat 19.17g 29% | Total Carbohydrates 10.3g 3% | Protein 2.58g 5%

Toscan Panzanella Salad Bowl

Servings: 5 | Preparation Time: 20 minutes

Ingredients

Bread

14 oz bread, cut into small pieces

2 Tbsp olive oil

1 tsp rosemary powder

1/2 tsp Maldon sea salt

Salad

5 tomatoes, chopped

1 large cucumber sliced

1 spring onion with green part sliced

2 Tbsp olive oil

2 Tbsp red wine vinegar

1 clove of garlic minced

1 tsp Maldon sea salt

1 Tbsp basil leaves (fresh, finely chopped)

Instructions

Bread

1. Preheat oven to 360 F/180 C.
2. Place the bread on a sheet lined with parchment paper.
3. Bake for about 10 minutes.
4. Transfer the bread into a bowl, season with the oil, the rosemary powder and Malodon sea salt; toss.

Salad

1. Add chopped tomatoes with all remaining ingredients and toss to combine well.
2. Cover and allow it to rest for 20 minutes.
3. Serve.

Nutrition Facts

Calories 341.64 | Total Fat 13.79g 21% | Total Carbohydrates 47.26g 16% | Protein 7.73g 15%

Vegan Noodles with Pesto

Servings: 4 | Preparation Time: 20 minutes

Ingredients

20 oz vegan noodles or spaghetti

Water, for boiling the noodles

Garlic Sauce

4 Tbsp coconut butter melted

2 to 3 Tbsp minced garlic

1 Tbsp Italian seasoning

1 Tbsp soy sauce

1 Tbsp hoisin sauce

1 Tbsp granulated sugar

Pine nuts and tomatoes for serving

Instructions

1. Cook noodles as per package directions.

2. Transfer the noodles in a colander to drain.

3. Add the coconut butter in a saucepan to melt; add all remaining ingredients and cook for 2 to 3 minutes, stirring constantly.

4. Transfer the garlic sauce into a small bowl.

5. Toss noodles with the garlic sauce and tomatoes to combine well.

6. Sprinkle with pine nuts and serve.

Nutrition Facts

Calories 617 | Total Fat 15.8g 25% | Total Carbohydrates 114.4g 38% | Protein 19.12g 38%

DINNER

Artichoke Hearts with Rice Bowl

Servings: 6 | Preparation Time: 40 minutes

Ingredients

1 cup of olive oil

10 artichoke hearts, canned, chopped

2 carrots cut into thin slices

1 cup of long-grain rice

3 cups vegetable broth

2 Tbsp fresh dill finely chopped

2 Tbsp fresh parsley finely chopped

2 Tbsp fresh lemon juice

Salt and ground pepper to taste

Instructions

1. Heat oil in a large saucepan over medium-high heat.

2. Add artichokes and cook for 5 minutes.

3. Add carrots and sauté for 2 to 3 minutes.

4. Add rice and stir for one minute.

5. Pour broth and add dill and parsley; stir.

6. Bring to a boil and reduce heat to simmer.

7. Cover and cook for 25 minutes over medium heat.

8. Stir in the fresh lemon juice and serve hot.

Nutrition Facts

Calories 445.61 | Total Fat 20.42g 31% | Total Carbohydrates 58g 20% | Protein 10.7g 21%

Broccoli Rabe, Crimini with Cannellini Beans Soup

Servings: 6 | Preparation Time: 35 minutes

Ingredients

2 Tbsp olive oil

2 medium onions finely chopped

4 cloves garlic, minced

Coarse salt and ground pepper

8 oz Cremini mushrooms trimmed and thinly sliced

1 lb broccoli rabe trimmed and coarsely chopped

2 cans of vegetable broth

1 cup of water

2 can (14 oz) of beans, washed and drained

2 Tbsp fresh parsley chopped

Instructions

1. In a large Dutch oven, warm oil over the medium heat.
2. Sauté onion and garlic for about 8 to 10 minutes.
3. Add mushrooms, and cook for 2 to 4 minutes.
4. Add broccoli rabe; cook for 2 to 3 minutes.
5. Add the vegetable broth and one cup of water; season with the salt and pepper.
6. Bring to a boil and reduce the heat to medium-low.
7. Cook, occasionally stirring, until the broccoli is tender, for 10 to 15 minutes.
8. Add beans and parsley; cook until warm, about 5 minutes.
9. Serve hot.

Nutrition Facts

Calories 303.84 | Total Fat 5.38g 8% | Total Carbohydrates 48g 16% | Protein 18.46g 37%

Fried Beans with Tofu Cheese Bowl

Servings: 3 | Preparation Time: 20 minutes

Ingredients

4 Tbsp sesame oil

1 lb green beans cut into pieces

1/2 lb tofu cheese extra-firm cut into cubes

2 Tbsp cooking wine

2 Tbsp soy sauce (or tamari sauce)

2 Tbsp toasted sesame seeds

Kosher salt and freshly ground black pepper, to taste

Instructions

1. Heat oil in a frying skillet over medium-high; add beans, and cook, often stirring, until tender, about 5 minutes.

2. Add the tofu cubes, stir and cook for a further 4 to 5 minutes.

3. Pour cooking wine and soy sauce; cook, stirring, until heated through, for about 3-4 minutes.

4. Remove from heat and stir in the sesame seeds; season with the salt and pepper.

5. Serve.

Nutrition Facts

Calories 293 | Total Fat 23.8g 37% | Total Carbohydrates 13.43g 4% | Protein 11.15g 22%

Lenten Rice, Mushrooms and Lettuce Bowl

Servings: 8 | Preparation Time: 30 minutes

Ingredients

3 Tbsp olive oil

2 lb fresh mushrooms cut into quarters

1 onion finely chopped

2 clove garlic minced

5 cups of vegetable broth

1 cup of glutinous rice

Salt and ground pepper to taste

1 medium head of lettuce chopped

1/2 bunch of fresh dill

4 to 5 spring onions sliced

Fresh juice of 1 lemon

1 lemon slices serving

Instructions

1. Heat oil in a pot over medium-high heat.

2. Sauté the onion, garlic, and mushroom for 5 minutes; stir occasionally.

3. Add the vegetable broth, rice, salt, pepper, cover, and simmer for 15 minutes.

4. Add lettuce, dill and spring onions to the pot and cook for a further 5 minutes.

5. Remove the pot from the heat and stir in the lemon juice.

6. Season to taste and serve with lemon slices.

Nutrition Facts

Calories 247.53 | Total Fat 8.29g 13% | Total Carbohydrates 36.34g 12% | Protein 10.18g 20%

Oven-baked Rice Stuffed Zucchini

Servings: 6 | Preparation Time: 1 hour and 5 minutes

Ingredients

2 lbs of small zucchini

6 Tbsp olive oil

1 onion finely chopped

2 cloves garlic minced

1 carrot grated

1 Tbsp of basil finely chopped

1 Tbsp fresh parsley finely chopped

1 cup of short-grain rice

2 1/2 cups of vegetable broth

Salt and ground pepper to taste

Instructions

1. Preheat oven to 360 F/180 C.

2. Wash and hollow out zucchini with the spoon; set aside.

3. Grease a baking dish with olive oil.

4. Heat oil in a frying skillet, and sauté the onion and garlic with the pinch of salt until soft.

5. Add the carrot, basil, and parsley; stir for about 2 minutes.

6. Add rice and vegetable broth and stir for 2 minutes.

7. Fill the zucchini with the rice mixture and place into prepared baking dish.

8. Cover with the foil and bake for 45 minutes.

9. Serve warm or cold.

Nutrition Facts

Calories 210.77 | Total Fat 14.2g 23% | Total Carbohydrates 16.9g 6% | Protein 4.8g 10%

PENNE PASTA WITH AVOCADO AND CORN SALAD

Servings: 6 | Preparation Time: 20 minutes

Ingredients

10 oz Penne pasta

Salt and ground pepper

20 cherry tomatoes halved

2 Tbsp fresh mint leaves chopped

2 Tbsp fresh basil chopped

3 Tbsp red vinegar

1/2 cup of olive oil

2 small avocados cut it into pieces

1 cup of canned corn

10 olives

20 g goji berries (optional)

Zest of 2 lemons

Fresh juice of 1 lemon

Basil leaves for serving

Instructions

1. Cook penne according to packet directions; rinse and set aside.

2. In a large bowl, add the cherry tomatoes, salt, pepper, mint, basil, vinegar, olive oil, and toss to combine well.

3. Add in avocado pieces and all remaining ingredients

4. Add the corn, olives, goji berries, lime zest and juice, one tablespoon mint, one tablespoon basil coarsely chopped, and mix.

5. Lightly stir with two wooden spoons.

6. Serve with the fresh basil leaves.

Nutrition Facts

Calories 473.81 | Total Fat 28.73g 44% | Total Carbohydrates 48g 16% | Protein 8.19g 16%

Peperonata - Southern Italian Pepper Salad

Servings: 3 | Preparation Time: 15 minutes

Ingredients

4 peppers (red, yellow, orange) seeded, cut into strips

4 Tbsp extra virgin olive oil

2 large cloves garlic minced

2 Tbsp red wine vinegar

1 Tbsp balsamic vinegar

1 tsp sugar

1 tsp kosher salt

Instructions

1. Cut the peppers into strips, and then the strips cut into 2 or 3 pieces.

2. In a large skillet, heat the oil and cook the minced garlic for 2 to 3 minutes.

3. Add the peppers and all remaining ingredients and stir well.

4. Cook over medium heat, occasionally stirring, until peppers soften completely.

5. Taste and adjust the salt.

6. Serve warm.

Nutrition Facts

Calories 220.54 | Total Fat 18.38g 28% | Total Carbohydrates 13.84g 5% | Protein 2.04g 4%

Red Cabbage Salad

Servings: 6 | Preparation Time: 15 minutes

Ingredients

1 lb red cabbage, finely chopped or shredded

1 onion red, sliced

2 garlic cloves, finely sliced

8 cherry tomatoes halved

1/2 cup olive oil

2 Tbsp of fresh lemon juice

1/2 tsp mustard seeds

1 Tbsp fresh cilantro coarsely chopped

Instructions

1. Rinse cabbage and clean from any dirt or yellow outer leaves.

2. Chop or shred cabbage and place in a large salad bowl.

3. Sprinkle with the salt and pepper; add the onion slices, halved cherry tomatoes, and garlic; toss to combine well.

4. In a small bowl, whisk the olive oil, lemon juice, mustard seeds, and cilantro

5. Pour dressing over cabbage salad, and toss to combine well. Serve.

Nutrition Facts

Calories 98.83 | Total Fat 3.49g 5% | Total Carbohydrates 16g 5% | Protein 3.14g 6%

Rice and Edamame with Citrus-Lime Vinaigrette Bowl

Servings: 4 | Preparation Time: 15 minutes

Ingredients

1 cup cooked brown rice

1 cup roasted vegetables (any)

1 cup edamame - immature soybeans in the pod

1 avocado, diced

2 Tbsp spring onions sliced

2 Tbsp fresh cilantro chopped

Citrus-Lime Vinaigrette

4 Tbsp olive oil

4 Tbsp fresh lime juice

4 Tbsp fresh orange juice

2 tsp jalapeno pepper minced

4 Tbsp fresh cilantro sliced

Salt and ground pepper to taste

Instructions

1. Arrange rice, vegetables, edamame, and avocado in a large salad bowl.

2. In a separate bowl, prepare the Citrus-Lime Vinaigrette.

3. Pour the vinaigrette evenly over the salad; lightly stir.

4. Serve.

Nutrition Facts

Calories 302.42 | Total Fat 17.34g 27% | Total Carbohydrates 33.05g 11% | Protein 7.9g 16%

Roasted Brussels Sprouts and Pumpkin Salad Bowl

Servings: 6 | Preparation Time: 40 minutes

Ingredients

Salad

1 lb Brussels sprouts

1 1/2 lbs pumpkin, without the peel and seeds, cut into cubes

1 fennel bulb, peeled

1 sweet potato, rinsed with the peel

1/2 lb broccoli cut into florets

4 Tbsp olive oil

Salt and ground pepper to taste

1 cup of whole walnuts

Dressing

1/2 cup of garlic-infused olive oil

4 to 5 Tbsp of Maple syrup

1/2 tsp cinnamon

Serving

Sun-dried tomatoes, drained and cut in halves

Instructions

1. Preheat the oven to 380 F/190 C.

2. Rinse and clean the Brussels sprouts and add them into a large bowl along with the pumpkin cubes.

3. Add the fennel, sweet potato, and broccoli florets.

4. Add the sweet potato and broccoli into the bowl.

5. Season with the salt and pepper, and pour the olive oil; toss to combine well.

6. Arrange the vegetables into two baking sheets lined with parchment paper.

7. Roast for about 20 minutes

8. In the last 10 minutes, add the walnuts and stir lightly.

9. Remove the baking pans from the oven.

10. Transfer the vegetables onto large salad bowl and season with the mixture of oil, Maple syrup, cinnamon, and the pinch of the salt and pepper; toss to combine.

11. Serve with sun-dried tomato halves.

Nutrition Facts

Calories 446.85 | Total Fat 40.3g 62% | Total Carbohydrates 25.83g 9% | Protein 7.51g 15%

Roasted Sweet Potato, Mushrooms & Pomegranate Bowl

Servings: 6 | Preparation Time: 1 hour and 10 minutes

Ingredients

Salad

3 lb sweet potatoes cut into large sliced

1 onion quartered

2 clove of garlic

1 Tbsp fresh rosemary

1 Tbsp fresh thyme

1 Tbsp oregano

1 lb oyster mushrooms

1 large head of green salad, chopped

1/2 pomegranate

1 Tbsp sunflower seeds

1 Tbsp fresh mint leaves chopped

Dressing

1/2 cup of balsamic vinegar

3/4 cup of olive oil

Salt and ground pepper

1 Tbsp paprika flakes

Instructions

1. Preheat oven to 390 F/185 C.

2. Peel the sweet potatoes, and cut them into large pieces, and place them into the baking pan along with onion and garlic.

3. Prepare the sauce and pour evenly over vegetables.

4. Place in oven and bake for 30 to 40 minutes.

5. Remove the hot baking pan from the oven, add the mushrooms, stir and bake for a further 15 to 20 minutes.

6. Remove the potato mixture from the oven and allow it to cool down for 10 minutes.

7. Cut the green salad and place it into a large salad bowl.

8. Add the sweet potato mixture and lightly stir.

9. Sprinkle with pomegranate, sunflower seeds, and fresh mint.

10. Drizzle with some olive oil and serve.

Nutrition Facts

Calories 321 | Total Fat 28.4g 44% | Total Carbohydrates 15.26g 5% | Protein 4g 8%

Spicy Asian Soup Bowl

Servings: 6 | Preparation Time: 30 minutes

Ingredients

Soup Base

1/4 cup of sesame oil

1 tsp of crushed chili pepper

3 dry red chili pepper

2 bay leaves

1 anise star

1 cinnamon stick

1 tsp of ground ginger

1/2 cup of cooking wine

4 to 5 cups of water

1 tsp of cumin seeds

1 tsp of sesame paste

1 Tbsp of soy sauce

Sea salt to taste

Soup ingredients

2 -3 lettuce leaves halved

1 cup of oyster mushrooms (or button mushrooms)

Coriander

Fried tofu cut into pieces

Instructions

1. Heat oil into a wok or frying skillet.

2. Fry a crushed chili peppers and red hot chili peppers.

3. Pour water (about 5 cups), and bring to boil.

4. Add all remaining ingredients for the soup base.

5. Cook for a further 10 to 12 minutes.

6. Add all soup ingredients and boil for a further 2 to 3 minutes.

7. Serve hot.

Nutrition Facts

Calories 144.15 | Total Fat 10.61g 16% | Total Carbohydrates 8.27g 3% | Protein 2.7g 6%

Sweet Potato Soup with Curry

Servings: 6 | Preparation Time: 50 minutes

Ingredients

2 Tbsp olive oil

2 onions finely chopped

1 clove garlic sliced

1 chili pepper finely sliced

1/2 cup of sundried tomatoes sliced

Salt and ground pepper to taste

1 Tbsp curry powder

1 Tbsp turmeric powder

1 Tbsp fresh thyme, finely chopped

2 lb sweet potatoes, rinsed and cut into cubes

4 cups of vegetable broth

1 1/2 cups of coconut milk

Fresh coriander for serving

Couscous for serving (optional)

Instructions

1. Heat the olive oil over medium heat.

2. Sauté the onion, garlic, and pepper with the pinch of salt and pepper for 2-3 minutes.

3. Add the curry, turmeric, thyme, sweet potatoes, and stir with a wooden spoon.

4. Pour vegetable broth, cover, and boil cook for 30 minutes over medium-low heat.

5. Stir in the coconut milk and boil for further 5 to10 minutes.

6. Remove from the heat, sprinkle with fresh coriander, and serve with couscous (optional).

Nutrition Facts

Calories 174.5 | Total Fat 13.38g 21% | Total Carbohydrates 12.17g 4% | Protein 5.5g 10%

Traditional Persian Shirazi Salad

Servings: 4 | Preparation Time: 15 minutes

Ingredients

5 Persian cucumbers cut into cubes

2 tomatoes, seeds removed, finely chopped

1/2 small red onion, finely chopped

1/2 cup fresh flat-leaf parsley, coarsely chopped

4 Tbsp extra-virgin olive oil

2 Tbsp fresh lemon juice

Kosher salt and freshly ground black pepper to taste

2 Tbsp dry mint for serving

Instructions

1. Add cucumbers, tomatoes, parsley, and red onions in a large salad bowl.

2. In a separate bowl, whisk together olive oil, lemon juice, and salt and pepper.

3. Pour dressing over the salad, sprinkle with mint and toss to combine well.

4. Refrigerate for at least one hour before serving.

Nutrition Facts

Calories 108.57 | Total Fat 10.3g 16% | Total Carbohydrates 4.34g 1% | Protein 0.78g 2%

Vegan Spicy Coconut Curry

Servings: 6 | Preparation Time: 35 minutes

Ingredients

4 Tbsp olive oil

1 onion finely chopped

4 potatoes, peeled and cut into pieces

2 cups of fresh spinach chopped

2 cups of fresh cauliflower flowerets

1 carrot grated

2 Tbsp spiced curry powder

1 tsp turmeric

1 cup tomato sauce

Salt and pepper to taste

1 can (11 oz) of coconut milk

Fresh coriander and lime for serving

Rice for serving (optional)

Instructions

1. In a large pot, heat the oil and sauté vegetables for a few minutes.
2. Add the curry powder, turmeric, tomato sauce, and 1 cup of water.
3. Season with salt and pepper, and cook for 15 minutes on medium heat.
4. Pour in the coconut milk, and cook for a further 10 minutes.
5. Remove from the heat and let it cool for 10 minutes.
6. Serve with rice, chopped fresh cilantro, and lime.

Nutrition Facts

Calories 264.94 | Total Fat 13.8g 21% | Total Carbohydrates 33.1g 11% | Protein 5.14g 10%

SNACKS

Avocado Guacamole Bowl

Servings: 10 | Preparation Time: 15 minutes

Ingredients

4 avocados peeled and seeded

1 small red onion diced

2 cloves of garlic finely chopped

1/2 cup of fresh cilantro finely chopped

4 jalapeno peppers seeded and finely diced

Fresh lime juice (about 2 limes)

Salt and freshly ground black pepper to taste

Lettuce, shredded for serving

Instructions

1. In a bowl, mash avocado with a potato masher or fork until chunky.

2. Add all remaining ingredients and stir with a fork.

3. Serve with tortilla chips.

4. Keep refrigerated in a bowl.

Nutrition Facts

Calories 153.89 | Total Fat 13.4g 21% | Total Carbohydrates 9.7g 3% | Protein 2.04g 4%

Baked Corn - Cashews Dip

Servings: 8 | Preparation Time: 30 minutes

Ingredients

1 1/2 cups of soaked cashews, drained

2 Tbsp olive oil

1 small onion finely chopped

1 tsp minced garlic

Sea salt and ground black pepper, to taste

3 cups fresh corn kernels or canned

1 small green pepper, seeded and chopped

2 Tbsp nutritional yeast

3/4 tsp cumin

4 Tbsp of almond milk

Instructions

1. Preheat oven to 380 F/190 C.
2. Heat olive oil in a large oven-safe skillet over medium-high heat.
3. Sauté the onion and garlic with a pinch of salt and pepper for about 3 minutes.
4. Add the fresh corn, and soaked cashews, and stir well.
5. Add all remaining ingredients and stir to combine well.
6. Bake for about 12 to 15 minutes or until bubbly.
7. Remove from the oven and allow it to cool for 5 minutes.
8. Serve in a bowl with pita bread, sliced vegetables, or tortilla chips.

Nutrition Facts

Calories 309.7 | Total Fat 18.27g 28% | Total Carbohydrates 33.16g 11% | Protein 10.07g 20%

Broccoli Mustard Dip

Servings: 6 | Preparation Time: 10 minutes

Ingredients

1/2 lb of broccoli flowerets cooked

1/2 cup of olive oil

2 Tbsp mustard (Dijon, English, ground stone)

1/2 cup lemon juice

2 clove garlic minced

2 Tbsp fresh basil leaves finely chopped

Salt and black pepper to taste

Instructions

1. Place all ingredients from the list in your fast-speed blender, and blend until the desired consistency is reached.

2. Serve in a bowl; keep refrigerated.

Nutrition Facts

Calories 183.46 | Total Fat 18.45g 28% | Total Carbohydrates 5.05g 2% | Protein 1.37g 3%

Creamy Cherry Salsa with Almonds

Servings: 6 | Preparation Time: 25 minutes

Ingredients

1/2 cup of canned cherry

1 cup of cherry syrup

1 cup of sugar

1/2 cup of water

3/4 cup of coconut cream

1/2 cup of toasted almonds sliced

Instructions

1. Cook cherries, the cherry syrup, and the sugar in a saucepan over medium heat for 20 minutes, often stir.

2. Remove from heat, add the coconut cream and stir to combine well.

3. Add almonds and stir again.

4. Allow it to cool down.

5. Serve with fresh fruits, bread, cookies etc.

Nutrition Facts

Calories 337.28 | Total Fat 16.46g 25% | Total Carbohydrates 48.27g 16% | Protein 3.79g 8%

Gluten-free Quinoa Bowl

Servings: 4 | Preparation Time: 20 minutes

Ingredients

1 cup of water

1 cup of quinoa

2 cups of coconut milk

2 Tbsp maple syrup

2 tsp chia seeds

1 pinch of salt

2 tsp raw cacao powder

Fresh fruits, coconut cream, nuts, dry fruits for topping

Instructions

1. Add water and cook quinoa in a pot over medium heat and bring to boil.

2. Cover the lid and let simmer for about 10 to 12 minutes, until all the water is absorbed.

3. Add coconut milk, maple syrup, chia seeds, salt, and cacao powder; stir to combine well.

4. Remove the heat and let the quinoa sit for about 10 minutes.

5. Transfer into bowls, garnish with your favorite topping and serve warm.

Nutrition Facts

Calories 367.69 | Total Fat 27.5g 43% | Total Carbohydrates 28.18g 9% | Protein 6.92g 14%

Hearty Black Bean Spread

Servings: 8 | Preparation Time: 10 minutes

Ingredients

1 can (15 oz) black beans drained, rinsed

1 bell pepper chopped

1 onion, coarsely chopped

1 garlic clove, chopped

1 Tbsp red wine vinegar

2 Tbsp olive oil

Freshly-ground black pepper, to taste

Instructions

1. Combine all ingredients in a food processor or blender.

2. Process or blend until the beans are coarsely mashed.

3. Place into a bowl and refrigerate before serving.

4. Serve with pita bread, bread, tortillas etc.

Nutrition Facts

Calories 99.24 | Total Fat 3.68g 6% | Total Carbohydrates 12.85g 4% | Protein 4.18g 8%

Instant Piquant Bean Dip

Servings: 6 | Preparation Time: 20 minutes

Ingredients

1 can (15 oz) of beans, drained

1 large onion finely chopped

1 to 2 mild chili peppers diced

2 Tbsp tomato puree

1 Tbsp balsamic vinegar (optional)

1 tsp garlic powder

6 Tbsp water

Salt to taste

Instructions

1. Add all ingredients into your Instant Pot and stir well.

2. Lock lid into place and set on the MANUAL setting high pressure for 12 minutes.

3. Release the switch to the Venting position and let the steam release quickly when the cooking time ends.

4. Transfer the bean mixture to your blender; blend until smooth.

5. Taste and adjust the salt to taste.

6. Serve in a bowl; keep refrigerated.

Nutrition Facts

Calories 90.1 | Total Fat 0.39g <1% | Total Carbohydrates 17g 6% | Protein 5.4g 11%

Italian Beans Hummus

Servings: 6 | Preparation Time: 10 minutes

Ingredients

1/4 cup of olive oil

2 garlic cloves finely chopped

1 can (15 oz) of Italian cannellini beans, drained

4 Tbsp sesame paste

3 Tbsp lemon juice freshly squeezed

2 Tbsp fresh basil chopped

2 Tbsp fresh parsley chopped

1/2 tsp red pepper flakes crushed

Salt to taste

Instructions

1. Place all ingredients in your food processor or into a blender.

2. Process until all ingredients combined well and until the desired consistency is reached.

3. Transfer mixture into a bowl and refrigerate before servings.

Nutrition Facts

Calories 42.21 | Total Fat 1.97g 3% | Total Carbohydrates 5.71g 2% | Protein 1.93g 4%

Parsley and Pine Nuts Dip

Servings: 6 | Preparation Time: 10 minutes

Ingredients

2 cups parsley leaves chopped

2 cloves garlic minced

1/3 cup lemon juice

4 Tbsp nutritional yeast

4 Tbsp water

1/3 cup extra virgin olive oil

Table salt to taste

Instructions

1. Add the parsley and all remaining ingredients in a blender or a food processor.

2. Blend until smooth or until the desired consistency is reached

3. Ready. Serve in a bowl.

Nutrition Facts

Calories 119.81 | Total Fat 12.23g 19% | Total Carbohydrates 2.81g <1% | Protein 0.97g 2%

Vegan Potato Salad

Servings: 6 | Preparation Time: 35 minutes

Ingredients

1 lb new red potatoes

4 Tbsp chopped scallions

3 celery stalks, chopped

1 red pepper, minced

4 Tbsp olive oil

2 Tbsp balsamic vinegar

1 Tbsp fresh parsley finely chopped

Salt and ground black pepper to taste

Instructions

1. Boil potatoes for 20 minutes in a large pot of boiling water.

2. Drain and let completely cool.

3. Cut potatoes into large chunks and toss the potatoes with the celery, red pepper, and scallions.

4. In a small bowl combine the oil, balsamic vinegar, chopped parsley, and the salt and ground black pepper to taste

5. Pour over potato mixture and toss to combine well.

6. Serve in a bowl immediately or keep refrigerated.

Nutrition Facts

Calories 122 | Total Fat 5g 8% | Total Carbohydrates 19g 6% | Protein 2g 4%

DESSERTS

Banana Apricot Cream Bowl

Servings: 3 | Preparation Time: 10 minutes

Ingredients

1 ripe banana frozen or fresh

2 apricots, cored, pitted, sliced

1 cup coconut milk (canned)

1/2 tsp vanilla extract

1/4 tsp ground cinnamon

Chopped apricot for serving

Instructions

1. Combine all ingredients into your high-speed blender.

2. Blend until smooth and combined well.

3. Serve into chilled bowls and cover with sliced apricots.

Nutrition Facts

Calories 152.58 | Total Fat 8.43g 13% | Total Carbohydrates 20.29g 7% | Protein 2.15g 4%

Coconut Cereals with Berry, Banana Bowl

Servings: 3 | Preparation Time: 15 minutes

Ingredients

5 Tbsp instant oat cereals

1 cup coconut milk canned

2 Tbsp coconut sugar

1 cinnamon stick

1 banana sliced

1 cup of berry mix (strawberries, raspberries, blueberries)

4 Tbsp walnuts chopped

1 Tbsp goji berry (optional)

Instructions

1. Add the oat flakes, coconut milk, coconut sugar, and cinnamon stick in a saucepan.

2. Bring to boil, reduce the heat to medium-low, and cook for about 5 minutes.

3. Pour the mixture in a bowl and remove the cinnamon stick.

4. Cover with banana slices, berry mix, and chopped walnuts.

5. Serve and enjoy!

Nutrition Facts

Calories 327| Total Fat 15.38g 24% | Total Carbohydrates 48g 16% |Protein 4.44g 9%

Coconut Yogurt Parfait with Berries

Servings: 2 | Preparation Time: 10 minutes

Ingredients

1 cup coconut yogurt or coconut cream

1/2 cup of cereals

1/2 cup of sliced strawberries

1/2 cup of blueberries

1/2 cup of raspberries

Instructions

1. Divide half of the coconut yogurt into bawls.

2. Cover with half of cereals and berries.

3. Spread over the remaining coconut yogurt and finish with cereals and berries.

4. Serve and enjoy!

Nutrition Facts

Calories 337.15 | Total Fat 25.72g 40% | Total Carbohydrates 25.9g 9% | Protein 6g 12%

Fruity Summer Smile Bowl

Servings: 6 | Preparation Time: 10 minutes

Ingredients

2 large bananas, sliced

2 cups fresh blueberries

2 cups strawberry slices

2 Tbsp Date syrup or simple syrup

1 fresh lime juice (about 2 limes)

1/2 cup pine nuts (optional)

Instructions

1. Combine bananas, blueberries, and strawberries in a bowl.

2. Drizzle syrup and lime juice evenly over fruit; stir to coat.

3. Sprinkle with pine nuts and serve.

Nutrition Facts

Calories 177.22 | Total Fat 8.18g 13% | Total Carbohydrates 27.5g 9% | Protein 2.7g 6%

Healthy Cocoa - Chia Cream

Servings: 4 | Preparation Time: 15 minutes

Ingredients

1/2 cup of Chia seeds

1 cup of coconut milk (canned)

2 Tbsp cocoa powder

1 tsp pure vanilla extract

1/4 cup of coconut palm sugar

1 cup of coconut cream (liquid expressed from grated meat)

Instructions

1. Add chia seeds, coconut milk, coconut powder, and vanilla extract in a mixing bowl.

2. Beat until the mixture combines well.

3. Add the coconut palm sugar, and beat until soft and creamy.

4. Divide the mixture into four bowls and chill for at least 2 hours.

5. Before serving, beat the coconut cream and pour over the chia seeds cream.

Nutrition Facts

Calories 374.85 | Total Fat 34.32g 53% | Total Carbohydrates 19.23g 6% | Protein 4.4g 9%

Japanese Shaved Matcha Ice Dessert

Servings: 3 | Preparation Time: 15 minutes

Ingredients

2 Tbsp of Matcha powder

1 cup of coconut cream

2 Tbsp coconut palm sugar

1 1/2 cups of crushed ice cubes

Instructions

1. In a bowl, stir the matcha powder with the coconut cream until smooth.

2. Add ice cubes in your high-speed blender; beat until the ice texture is like snow.

3. Pour the matcha mixture evenly over the shaved ice.

4. Serve in chilled bowl or glasses.

Nutrition Facts

Calories 307.04 | Total Fat 28.24g 43% | Total Carbohydrates 16.4g 5% | Protein 3.62g 7%

Murky Acai Banana Bowl

Servings: 2 | Preparation Time: 10 minutes

Ingredients

3 to 4 Acai fruit pulp

1 Tbsp granulated sugar

2 bananas sliced

1 Tbsp of dark cocoa nibs

4 ice cubes crushed

2 Tbsp of granola (optional)

Instructions

1. Add acai pulp in a blender along with sugar, one banana, cocoa nibs, and crushed ice.

2. Blend until combined well.

3. Pour the acai mixture into a bowl; add banana slices and granola on a top.

4. Enjoy!

Nutrition Facts

Calories 215 | Total Fat 2.84g 4% | Total Carbohydrates 49g 17% | Protein 3.49g 7%

Pumpkin Parfait with Coconut Nibs Bowl

Servings: 6 | Preparation Time: 15 minutes

Ingredients

1 can (14 oz) of pumpkin puree

1/2 tsp pumpkin pie spice

Pinch of salt

2 cups silken tofu, soft

1 cup icing sugar

1 cup of coconut cream

1/2 cup of cacao nibs

Instructions

1. In a bowl, beat the pumpkin puree, spice, salt, 1 cup of silken tofu, and 1/2 cup of icing sugar until smooth.

2. In a separate bowl, beat the coconut cream, 1 cup of silken tofu and 1/2 cup icing sugar until combined well.

3. Put in the bowls/glasses the layers - pumpkin mixture, coconut mixture, and nibs; repeat the layers.

4. Refrigerate for at least 1 hour.

5. Serve.

Nutrition Facts

Calories 236 | Total Fat 18.66g 29% | Total Carbohydrates 15.18g 5% | Protein 5.27g 11%

Quinoa-Banana Monkey Bowl

Servings: 2 | Preparation Time: 15 minutes

Ingredients

2 sliced banana

1/2 cup blackberries and blueberries mix

1 Tbsp dark cocoa nibs

4 Tbsp quinoa cooked

2 Tbsp almond butter

1 Tbsp Maple syrup or date syrup

1 Tbsp sliced almonds

Instructions

1. Add one sliced banana along with all remaining ingredients in a blender; blend until combined well.

2. Place another sliced banana at the bottom of a bowl, and pour with the toppings.

3. Serve immediately.

Nutrition Facts

Calories 304.6 | Total Fat 15.09g 23% | Total Carbohydrates 43.9g 15% | Protein 4.12g 8%

Vegan 'Cotton Candy' Mousse

Servings: 4 | Preparation Time: 10 minutes

Ingredients

1 cup of silken tofu soft

2 Tbsp Maple syrup

1 cup of coconut cream

1 cup of powdered sugar

1 cup of frozen strawberries

Instructions

1. Add all ingredients into your standing mixer; beat until soft and creamy.

2. Spoon into dessert bowls/glasses or any small serving dishes.

3. Chill for at least 2 hours.

4. Serve cold.

Nutrition Facts

Calories 266 | Total Fat 22.28g 34% | Total Carbohydrates 15.69g 5% | Protein 4.84g 10%

BRUNCH

Exotic Fruit Salad with Lime Syrup

Servings: 5 | Preparation Time: 15 minutes

Ingredients

2 cups of fresh berries mix

3 kiwis, peeled, sliced

1 mango, peeled, pitted, sliced

1/2 cup coconut palm sugar (or granulated sugar)

1/4 cup coconut water

1 Tbsp lime zest (from 1 lime)

2 Tbsp lime juice freshly squeezed

Instructions

1. Arrange the berries, kiwi, and mango in a salad bowl.

2. Combine the coconut sugar and lime zest in a saucepan and bring to boil over medium heat.

3. Remove from the heat and stir in the lime juice.

4. Pour the warm syrup over the fruit salad and gently toss.

5. Cover and refrigerate for about 2 hours.

6. Serve.

Nutrition Facts

Calories 143.39 | Total Fat 0.56g <1% | Total Carbohydrates 36.75g 12% | Protein 1.27g 3%

Fruit Bowl with Poppy Seeds

Servings: 3 | Preparation Time: 10 minutes

Ingredients

1 large banana

1 orange sliced

1/2 pomegranate

1 kiwi sliced

1/4 cup of walnuts, halved

2 Tbsp Maple syrup (optional)

2 Tbsp ground poppy seeds

Instructions

1. Arrange fruits and walnuts into a large salad bowl.

2. Drizzle with the Maple syrup and sprinkle with poppy seeds; toss to combine well.

3. Serve immediately.

Nutrition Facts

Calories 222.2 | Total Fat 9.32g 14% | Total Carbohydrates 34.6g 12% | Protein 4.11g 8%

Fruity Couscous Salad

Servings: 4 | Preparation Time: 15 minutes

Ingredients

1 cup couscous, cooked

1 cup of strawberries halves

1 peach diced

3 to4 plums sliced

2/3 cup slivered almonds

2 Tbsp Maple syrup

Instructions

1. Prepare couscous according to manufacturer directions.

2. Arrange fruits on a salad bowl with the couscous.

3. Pour Maple syrup evenly over the salad.

4. Serve.

Nutrition Facts

Calories 375.72 | Total Fat 12.61g 19% | Total Carbohydrates 57.39g 19% | Protein 11.3g 23%

Quinoa and Fruits Salad Bowl

Servings: 4 | Preparation Time: 25 minutes

Ingredients

1 cup quinoa soaked overnight

2 cups of water

1/2 tsp salt

2 cups of fresh vegetable mix

1 small avocado sliced

1/2 cup of corn kernels, canned

1 peach sliced

1 orange sliced

1 Tbsp chia seeds

Instructions

1. Rinse soaked quinoa under running water.

2. Place quinoa in a pot and cook with salted water; bring to boil, and cook for 12 minutes.

3. Add fruits and corn in a large salad bowl.

4. Stir in quinoa and add in a salad bowl.

5. Sprinkle with the chia seeds and serve.

Nutrition Facts

Calories 298.3 | Total Fat 12.2g 19% | Total Carbohydrates 40.1g 14% | Protein 8.67g 17%

Watermelon Fruit Salad Bowl

Servings: 6 | Preparation Time: 15 minutes

Ingredients

2 cups of watermelon, seeded and cut into cubes

2 cups of melon, seeded and cut into cubes

1 apple, peeled and cut into cubes

1 peach, peeled and cut into cubes

A handful of fresh blueberries

4 Tbsp coconut sugar (granulated sugar will work too)

1 to 2 Tbsp lemon juice (freshly squeezed)

Instructions

1. Combine all fruits in a large mixing bowl, and sprinkle with coconut palm sugar; toss.

2. Drizzle evenly with the lemon juice.

3. Cover and refrigerate for 2 hours.

4. Toss and serve.

Nutrition Facts

Calories 73.46 | Total Fat 0.25g <1% | Total Carbohydrates 19.59g 7% | Protein 0.82g 2%

ABOUT THE AUTHOR

Joseph P. Turner has spent his life learning what makes a healthy lifestyle and how to train our bodies to achieve maximum potential. What makes his journey more incredible is he has learned how to do all this while being vegan. He believes that we can each achieve optimum health without compromising our core values and maintaining a healthy lifestyle without the chemicals and preservatives that go into most good. His healthy living approach is both simple and easy to maintain.

His first book is the Meatless Power Cookbook for Vegan Athletes. It focuses on his own personal recipes as well as several he has discovered over the years to trim the fat, lose weight, and feel good in the process.

Joseph is a certified fitness trainer and nutritionist. When he is not in the gym Joseph can be found hard at work in the kitchen whipping up his favorite meals or creating new, delicious dishes. Writing may be his latest endeavor, but cooking has always been his true passion.

Your Free Gift

LINK ON THE BOOK: **BIT.LY/VEGAN-BONUS-BOOK** OR SCAN QR CODE BELOW

Other Books by Joseph P. Turner

Meatless Power Cookbook For Vegan Athletes

https://geni.us/vegan-athletes

Vegan Meal Prep Cookbook for Athletes

https://geni.us/vegan-meal-prep

One Last Thing...

DID YOU ENJOY THE BOOK?

IF SO, THEN LET ME KNOW BY LEAVING A REVIEW ON AMAZON! Reviews are the lifeblood of independent authors. I would appreciate even a few words and rating if that's all you have time for

IF YOU DID NOT LIKE THIS BOOK, THEN PLEASE TELL ME! Email me at perfectecruz@gmail.com and let me know what you didn't like! Perhaps I can change it. In today's world, a book doesn't have to be stagnant; it can improve with time and feedback from readers like you. You can impact this book, and I welcome your feedback. Help make this book better for everyone!

Printed in Great Britain
by Amazon